Start TO Finish
Second Series

Nature's Cycles

FROM Tadpole TO Frog

SHANNON ZEMLICKA

LERNER PUBLICATIONS COMPANY · Minneapolis

Photo Acknowledgments
The images in this book are used with the permission of: © Harry Rogers/Photo Researchers, Inc., pp. 1, 11, 19; © Kevin Snair/SuperStock, p. 3; © Jim Merli/Visuals Unlimited, Inc., p. 5; © NHPA/SuperStock, p. 7; © Barrie Watts/Alamy, p. 9; © Minden Pictures/SuperStock, p. 13; © John Mitchell/Photo Researchers, Inc., pp. 15, 17; © Animals Animals/SuperStock, p. 21; © David Aubrey/Photo Researchers, Inc., p. 23.

Front cover: © Jason Patrick Ross/Shutterstock Images.

Lerner Publications Company
A division of Lerner Publishing Group, Inc.
241 First Avenue North
Minneapolis, MN 55401 U.S.A.

Website address: www.lernerbooks.com

Library of Congress Cataloging-in-Publication Data

Knudsen, Shannon, 1971–
    From tadpole to frog / by Shannon Zemlicka.
        p.   cm. — (Start to finish, second series: nature's cycles)
    Includes index.
    ISBN 978-0-7613-6565-5 (lib. bdg. : alk. paper)
    1. Frogs—Life cycles—Juvenile literature. I. Title.
QL668.E2Z465 2012
597.8'9—dc23   2011024572

Manufactured in the United States of America
1 – DP – 12/31/11

TABLE OF Contents

Ribbit! Here is a frog. How does a frog grow?

A tiny animal grows.

A mother frog lays many eggs. Some kinds of frogs lay eggs on land. Most kinds lay eggs underwater. Thick goo covers the eggs to protect them. A tiny animal grows inside each egg.

The tadpole leaves the egg.

The tiny animal grows for about a month. Then it breaks out of its egg. This is called **hatching**. Now the animal is a tadpole. A tadpole looks like a small, black fish. It breathes with body parts called **gills**.

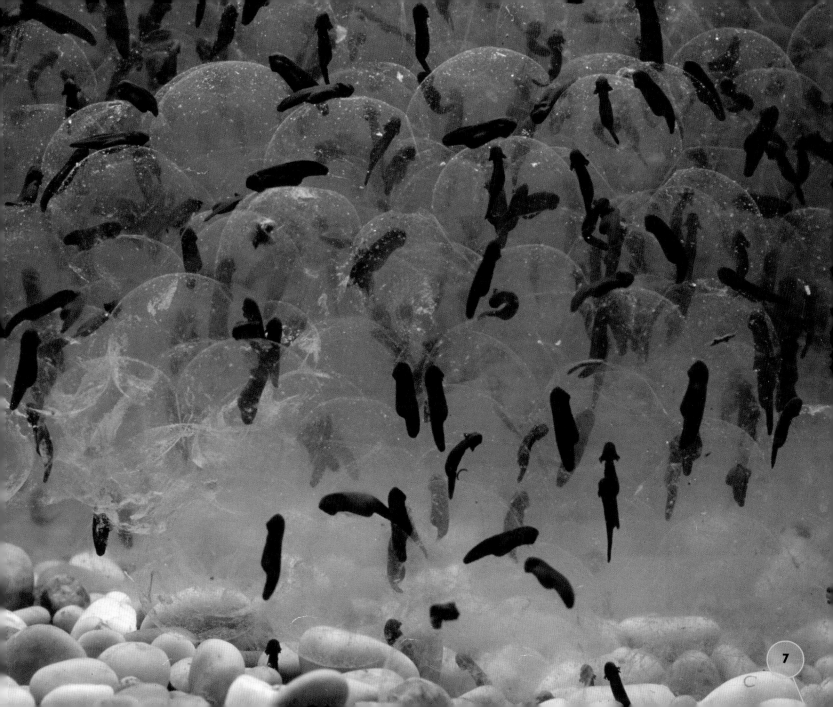

The tail gets longer.

The young tadpole is small and weak. It cannot swim yet. The tadpole holds on to a plant or a rock with its mouth. Its tail begins to grow.

The tadpole starts to swim.

The tadpole wiggles its tail to swim. Swimming makes the tadpole hungry. What will it do?

The tadpole starts to eat.

The tadpole eats tiny plants that grow underwater. Some tadpoles also eat frog eggs. Some tadpoles even eat other tadpoles! Eating makes the tadpole grow.

Back legs grow.

Two tiny bumps appear near the tadpole's tail. The bumps grow into back legs. The tadpole kicks its back legs to help it swim.

Front legs grow.

Two more bumps appear near the tadpole's head. These bumps grow into front legs. **Lungs** begin to grow inside the tadpole's body. Lungs let the tadpole breathe air.

The tadpole leaves the water.

The tadpole has legs for hopping and walking. It has lungs for breathing air. It can live on land. It climbs out of the water and becomes a **froglet**.

The tail shrinks.

The froglet catches insects to eat on land. Some kinds of froglets also catch food in the water. A froglet swims with its legs. It does not need a tail to swim. The tail slowly shrinks.

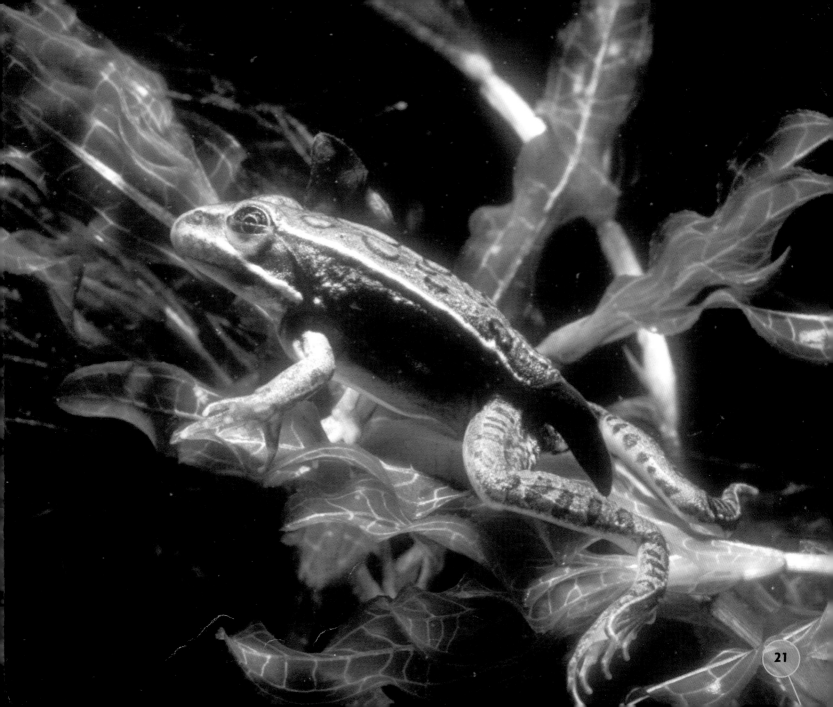

Hello, frog!

The froglet becomes a frog when its tail is gone. It has grown from tadpole to frog!

Glossary

froglet (FRAWG-leht): a frog's form when it has left the water and still has a tail

gills (GIHLZ): body parts for breathing underwater

hatching (HACH-ing): breaking out of an egg

lungs (LUHNGZ): body parts for breathing air

tadpole (TAD-pohl): a frog's form after it leaves an egg

Index